t l

IRON
PRESS

This edition first published 2015 by
IRON Press, 5 Marden Terrace
Cullercoats, North Shields
Tyne & Wear NE30 4PD
Tel: +44(0)191 2531901
ironpress@blueyonder.co.uk
www.ironpress.co.uk

First edition printed 1992
Second print 1992
Third print 1994
Fourth print 1996
Fifth print 1999
Sixth print 2002

Edited by Peter Mortimer

Printed by Ingram / Lightning Source
ISBN 978-0-9931245-0-1
Cover design Kate Jones

IRON Press books are distributed by Central Books
and represented by Inpress Ltd
Churchill House, 12 Mosley Street,
Newcastle upon Tyne, NE1 1DE
tel: +44(0)191 2308104
www.inpressbooks.co.uk

Introduction

THIS COLLECTION WAS FIRST PUBLISHED IN 1992 AND proved to be one of several watersheds not only for IRON Press, but for the haiku form in the UK and also for the British Haiku Society which had been formed two years previously, with its first president, the eminent poet James Kirkup. The formation of BHS took place on the eve of the international haiku contest organised by the Welsh Academy, Cardiff in 1991, which attracted 1,500 entries. It's worth recording the three main prizes went to BHS members, David Cobb, Jackie Hardy and Dee Evetts.

A momentum was growing and David Cobb approached IRON Press to see if we were interested in putting together an anthology to celebrate the first British Haiku Event – the largest event of its kind ever seen in the UK. This attracted 5,500 submissions.

It was from this impressive group that David, myself and James Kirkup, (who died in May 2009) finally forged this current collection.

Between us we whittled down the haiku to one hundred which originally IRON Press planned to print as a pamphlet to be given away free to subscribers renewing with IRON Magazine (the magazine ran for 83 editions from 1973 to 1997). David Parrish, the director of our then distributor Password Books, persuaded us instead to do it as a mini book, perfect bound with a spine. It was A7 in size – a nightmare for any printer to trim.

We had no idea then that the collection would prove so popular. Over the next ten years it ran to no fewer than six prints and around 10,000 copies, making it the biggest selling book of English language haiku published in the UK – also the smallest size book IRON Press had ever published. Something about its size and spirit seemed to appeal to people who liked to keep it in a top pocket or handbag, reading a dozen or so haiku while waiting at the bus stop, taking a coffee break or commuting into work.

The British Haiku Society proved to be a highly active force and David Cobb instigated a good deal of work in schools and elsewhere. The BHS has its own magazine Blithe Spirit (inspired by the British writer, quirky academic and great advocate of haiku in the west, R.H. Blyth). This was first edited by Jackie Hardy, followed by Caroline Gourley, Graham High, Mark

Rutter, Colin Blundell and now (in its silver jubilee year) David Serjeant. It has a membership approaching 300.

Part of haiku's growing appeal in the UK was the fact it carried little of the mistrust the public had of much modern poetry, which they either failed to understand or to relate to. Good haiku, though it could be intellectually challenging, was never obscurantist, relying as it did on strong and concrete imagery. It has proved especially popular in schools where the pupils readily take it on. Haiku was a favourite of the Beat Generation and has close links to Zen Buddhism, though it's true to say some modern poets hate it.

This book has been due for a rebirth for some time, but the pressures on a small press have previously made this new edition impossible. At last it is now published, with a new format, size, introduction and design, though with every original haiku intact. We also republish the children's haiku section, even though those young scribes will have been adults for some years.

We would be delighted to hear from many of the authors who, in the intervening twenty-three years, are no longer contactable. This would enable us to send them complimentary copies.

IRON Press has published a large range of haiku since *The Haiku Hundred* first saw the light of day and often in close co-operation with the BHS and David Cobb in particular. There have been several straightforward collections, plus *Venice Haiku* (Mike Wilkin), *Film Haiku* (Mick Haining), and two collections each spanning a year in the writer's life, *Thinking Once a Week* (Colin Stewart Jones) and *Our Sweet Little Time* (Hamish Ironside). As well as being a tireless activist for the form, David Cobb is also one of its most talented practitioners and we have been delighted to make use of those talents. He has been an editor or co-editor of various haiku anthologies for us and author of his own IRON Press collection, the haiku sequence, *Jumping from Kiyomitzu*.

Our international haiku anthologies, *The IRON Book of British Haiku*, *Euro Haiku* and *Global Haiku* have all included introductions addressing the subject of just what does and does not constitute a haiku in modern western society. There is no rule book on this, be it regarding the traditional 5-7-5 syllables (which we feel writers can adhere to or not), a reference to the seasons (ditto), the number of lines or whatever, (we did include some one line haiku). Haiku traditionally always steered clear of straight sentiment or feeling, but again this aspect was challenged in the IRON Press anthology edited by David Cobb, *The Humours of Haiku*. Whenever the product of one culture is absorbed into another, there are changes. We should not be insular about this. How many people realise the sonnet is originally from Italy?

Haiku's history is complex but in its modern form it first came into being in 17th century Japan, a country which has remained its traditional home. Purists think that's where it should stay, but it's always more exciting to mix things up a bit. No-one seriously believes football would have been better off staying in England, (though it might have saved us a few humiliations). National haiku societies now exist across the globe and learned academics regularly gather together for haiku conferences. Our anthology *Global Haiku* (co-published by the Canadian Mosaic Press) was actually launched at a haiku academic conference in the USA which adopted the same name, Global Haiku. Haiku is linked to several related but different forms such as senryu, tanka and haibun. IRON Press has published all these forms though our tendency (for better or worse) has been to concentrate on haiku itself. It's argued (by David Cobb for one) that the development of and growing interest in both haiku and these other forms makes *The Haiku Hundred* now merely an historical curiosity. Which may be true and nothing stands still, but literature is not merely the current moment and many people we're certain will be interested to see this collection with its original contents intact. Those interested in reading what David Cobb has to say on this growing interest in haibun and senryu in the country might wish to go to <www.davidcobb.co.uk>.

We have had some fun with haiku here in our two recent festivals. *The IRON Age 2013*, (celebrating the press's first forty years) and *Eclectic IRON 2015*, (celebrating the fact the first festival was such a success). In 2013 we programmed a day of Sea Haiku trips, poets sent out on the boat with the Cullercoats fisherman John

Stocks to see what the odysseys might produce (plans were partially scuppered by atrocious weather). In 2015 we organised Baiku, where a clutch of poets set off on a 20 mile bike ride through countryside and along the coast, likewise to see the effect on their creative juices. The expeditions were followed by haiku workshops, Sea Haiku run by David Cobb himself and Baiku run by the Liverpool poet David Bateman. Plans for small haiku collections from these events are still alive.

These IRON Press activities – plus several more – evolved from the publication of this little book in 1992. It is both a period piece and of contemporary relevance. As such, we are delighted finally to see it back in print and hope it stands the test of time and that haiku will continue to help keep contemporary poetry refreshed and on its toes.

This new edition is published solely by IRON Press and is not connected to the British Haiku Society.

Peter Mortimer
Editor, IRON Press
Cullercoats 2015

the haiku
100

Well before midnight
on my watch face tomorrow's
date already here

David Andrew

The echo of guests:
two apples blush alone on
the white tablecloth.

Kevin Bailey

old cemetery
all the sprinklers going
in the pouring rain

Winona Baker

watching my daughter
watching her daughter washing
her doll's white socks

Louise Beavan

On the beach at dawn –
last night's heart
washed clean away.

David Bell

train whistle
stretched on thin night air
across the river

Mary Lou Bittle-De Lapa

as stars are fading
a galaxy of freckles
on your sleeping back

Elizabeth Bletsoe

Redundant Deeside
Tank wagons shunted through grass
Locked brakes pinned in rust

John Calvert

This long recession:
At the end of my tee-square
A spider starts work.

Brian Cater

the porch light beckons –
the old toad in the shadow
waits, with lifted head

Tessa Rose Chester

after the fall
seeing the rooks wheel round
behind the poplars

David Cobb

the purple poppy
turns its head
at each breath of wind

Ion Codrescu

A rug of violets
vies for a place to push up
through rusted bed-springs.

C. Coiffait

A thin envelope
on the mat; my name in black.
How cold the hallway!

Geoffrey Daniel

A gull circles
over the halfmoon
bay.

Joan Daniels

Autumn sunlight
the tooled leather of the table
as I write

Adele Davide

stepping swiftly
across hot sand to the place
where the goats eat cardboard

Ian Duckett

The star, that wanders
Out of its constellation,
Is an aeroplane.

Tom Earley

sunday-morning sex
lasts only as long as the
children's video

Gerald England

home after dark
through the window my family
of strangers

Dee Evetts

The fluttering handkerchief
turns into seagull
to follow the ship

Feyyaz Fergar

sunburnt cheek –
from watching the geese
go west

Alec Finlay

Unfocused landscape –
windows curtained with rain.
    Days
leaking into days.

Andrew Gibbons

a stumble
shifts a rock
putting the beck
out of tune

Harry Gilonis

lightning falls on the farmhouse –
for a moment
the chickens see the fox

John Gonzalez

June moon …
rivulet of dog-piddle
intrigues the cat

Richard Goring

in the silent movie
a bird I think extinct
is singing

LeRoy Gorman

hunting-spider
on the doorpost – tense
to my key in the lock

Philip Gross

silent life
an inch below the surface
   carp come and go

Michael Gunton

birthday shopping –
into the dress she loves
her daughter's hips

Lee Gurga

on three faces
the same nose:
family snapshot

William Hart

yanked from the clothesline
the sound of the sheet
becoming wind

Christopher Herold

autumn night
Orion's bow releasing
arrows of geese

Anna Holley

A twig of raindrops.
Straphangers on a branch line
getting off shortly.

Geoffrey Holloway

another day of snow –
the statue's fingers
broken off

Gary Hotham

candlelight –
a shadow
turns the page

Brian David Johnston

fox sparrow
disturbing dead leaves …
reading your epitaph

Brian David Johnston

heavy with child
    farm wife carefully
    gathers the eggs

Jean Jorgensen

staff party
   hand on his wife's back
   while his eyes wander

Jean Jorgensen

midsummer morning –
the dead tree's shadow
stretches upstream

Adele Kenny

hauled up on deck
the humpback whale
breathing its own blood

Adele Kenny

On the verandah
the wet-nurse thinks of her own
pomegranate-tree.

Mimi Khalvati

big dragonfly eyes
either side of a grass blade
watching intruders

Marianne Kiauta

Mountain berries ripe –
even the droppings of birds
are a deep purple

James Kirkup

In the village pond
the full moon is shaken by
the first falling leaf

James Kirkup

Parting –
note on table,
cup still warm.

David Lawson

Old man dies —
on his wrist
seconds tick on.

David Lawson

after the rain —
milking the wet cow,
its body steaming

David LeCount

empty field –
chalked soccer lines
whiten the wind …

David LeCount

smoky spotlight –
the naked dancer
pops her bubblegum

Kenneth Leibman

Swallows nest under
the railway bridge: beneath them
a cardboard city.

Tony Lewis-Jones

On the VDU,
a bright ray of sunshine falls,
and the message fades.

John Light

Master of the marsh
– setting his trap
in the middle of the moon

Matthew Louviere

the champagne bottle
decked with roses and ribbons
awaits the midday tide

James McEwan

reflecting
      in the shadowed room
eye of the rockinghorse

Anne McKay

sixteen floors up
on the window ledge
a grasshopper

Marianne Monaco

The midnight train chases
a beam of moonlight
its shadow following

Eric Morgan

the old corral
corrals
a snow drift

Joanne Morcom

the wind
has no sound
but each leaf ...

Chris Mulhern

winter twilight ...
news vendor's change
icy in my hand

Patricia Neubauer

doll hospital –
the man brings out a tray
of new blue eyes

Patricia Neubauer

at ten thousand feet
opening the hamper
a monarch butterfly

Greer Newcomb

Punctuating
our love-making
– a single cigarette

Stuart Nind

You walking ahead
the grass springing back
erases your steps

Jim Norton

hot bath water
cold on the breastless side
another fine day

Yoko Ogino

Spider's web
delicately flapping
alongside the washing.

Eileen O'Hara

Puffing up dust
        as it follows a toad
the dog's nose.

Colin Oliver

On the lowest branch
        the sparrow shrieks
at the sleeping cat.

Colin Oliver

Morning mist dissolves,
overhead a skein of geese;
red haws glint in sun.

Constance Parr

Full to capacity
a pair of men's trousers
blowing in the wind.

Cy Patterson

Gift amaryllis
forgotten behind cupboards
punches through its carton.

Peggy Poole

drawing a house
with a fenced-in yard
the deaf boy

Francine Porad

Twenty-one dolphins
danced in the harbour
the teacher kept talking

James Potts

Two sparrows squabble
over some crumbs …
Tomorrow
I draw my pension.

Dan Pugh

A growing shadow
on my dusty lungs – the sun
shines on the mountain.

Dylan Pugh

guest towel
    draped on bathside:
        unused

A.G. Purkis

As the sun sets behind me
   my long shadow tells me
the way I must go

Dudley Reeves

after the storm
the child pulling a wagon
of rain

Marlina Rinzen

in the autumn dusk
the parrot repeats the name
of its dead master

Kohjin Sakamoto

drawn by the cries
of the winging wild geese
the blind dog's gaze

Kohjin Sakamoto

The dancer's gesture
   extends
      beyond her fingers

Eric Speight

caterpillars
  nibbling away
    my shade

Ruby Spriggs

i shout
at my son   the mountain
shouts back

George Swede

in the dentist's waiting room
  tulips with their petals
    tightly shut

George Swede

in parting
   the moon in a puddle
      shattered

Brian Tasker

Snowflakes are falling
covering all things except
the shape of your name

Cecily Taylor

Pregnant cat's
eyes follow me
everywhere

Tsunehiko Hoshino

The small jar
has bent
the gold fish.

Hamish Turnbull

ram's skull
neatly slotted
into a drystone wall

Walter Watson

old man
rolling a melon
autumn rain

Nina Wicker

with the haiku rejection
a long strand
of dark grey hair

Jonas Winet

between the pages
of a favourite book I find
squashed fruit-cake crumbs

Annie Wright

Children's Section

All alone again
  Standing by the river side
    And the wind nearby.

Jacqueline Johnston (13)

Train shoots past,
Passengers inside
Supping their tea.

Deborah Bow (13)

Still the bird stands
Watching the worm
Fight its way through the earth.

Shirley Rennick (13)

The green grass glistens
in the deep crimson sunset.
A flower shivers.

Charlotte Gidman (12)

Children everywhere
Teachers angry and shouting
Bell goes; not a sound

Alice Hambleton (12)

The dead leaves are falling

they look like my heart.

Mitsue Maeda (13)

They tell me the stars
are sky fire; to me, they remain
    silent sopranos.

Zoe Redgrove (14)

Cat: He grabbed a poem
    out of the air.
His tailed waved it in semaphore.

Zoe Redgrove (14)

Lightning Source UK Ltd.
Milton Keynes UK
UKOW06f0255270815

257624UK00008B/81/P